Rookie STAR™
Fact Finder

D1021396

10 Fascinating Facts About

Chewing Gum

by Jessica Cohn

Content Consultant

Nanci R. Vargus, Ed.D.
Professor Emeritus, University of Indianapolis

Reading Consultant

Jeanne M. Clidas, Ph.D.
Reading Specialist

Children's Press®
An Imprint of Scholastic Inc.

Table of Contents

Chewing gum has been a popular treat for a long time. Did you know that scientists found a wad of gum that was thousands of years old? THOUSANDS!

Do you want to learn more fascinating facts about gum? Then read on!

The first gum
came from trees

John B. Curtis (right) experimented with tree resin (below) to make gum.

For years, people chewed the soft parts of trees— nature's gum! Then in 1848, John B. Curtis boiled the **resin** from a spruce tree. He hardened the

resin in ice water. Then he formed it into sticks and wrapped them up. The first chewing gum was ready to sell! It was called State of Maine Pure Spruce Gum.

Monkeys and apes chew tree gum. And that's not all! The **primates** also have been known to stick gum in their hair. Nobody knows why!

There are more than 1,000 flavors

In 1884, a man named Thomas Adams made licorice gum. That was the most popular flavor at

Fruity and minty gums are pretty common. There are unusual flavors, too—like bacon, pickles, and turkey dinner.

the time. Today mint is most popular. And there are more than 1,000 other choices!

The inventor of bubble gum made it pink because that was the only color he had in his lab. For a long time, it stayed that way. Now bubble gum comes in a rainbow of colors!

9

There is a brand that perfumes your skin

Chewing gum can make breath smell better. But gum makers in Japan have gone one step further.

The perfume gums make you smell like lemons or roses.

ASIA

Japan

N

W · E

S

PACIFIC OCEAN

They make gum that works like perfume! After you chew it, the smell comes out of your skin.

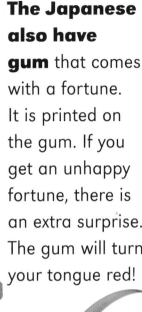

The Japanese also have gum that comes with a fortune. It is printed on the gum. If you get an unhappy fortune, there is an extra surprise. The gum will turn your tongue red!

Chomping can be a healthy habit

Chewing gum causes more spit to enter the mouth. The saliva helps protect the teeth from rotting.

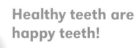

Healthy teeth are happy teeth!

Some scientists say that gum can help keep us happy, too. It makes us feel calm.

Chewing gum can also stop head pain when you fly. When you are in the air, your ears may feel clogged. Your head might hurt. Chewing gum makes you swallow more, which can help fix that feeling.

Chewing uses a lot of energy

Have you ever chewed gum so long it made your jaw hurt? All that gnawing takes **energy**. The amount of energy used by people around the world who chew gum each day is shocking. It could light a city of 10 million people for a day!

Imagine chewing long enough to light up a city!

GUINNESS WORLD RECORDS

The world record for the most people chewing gum at any one time was set in 2014. On that day, 747 people in Madrid, Spain, chewed gum at the same time.

The biggest piece was the size of a kid

Willie Mays is one of the best baseball players ever. But in 1974, he was known for something else—owning

Mays hit 660 home runs in his major-league career.

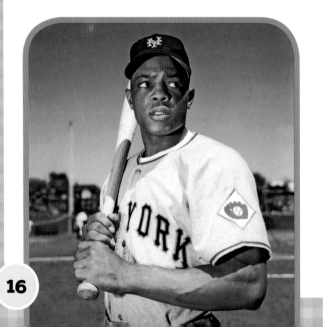

the biggest piece of gum ever! That year Mays visited a company that made gum. The workers gave him a piece that weighed more than 50 pounds. That's as much as 10,000 pieces!

What was the size of the biggest bubble? Do you think it was five inches? Maybe 10? It was 20 inches (50.8 centimeters). Chad Fell set the world record in 2004—with no hands!

20 inches
(50.8 centimeters)

Americans make the most chewing gum

This graph shows how much gum the four biggest makers produce.

On average, Americans chew nearly 300 sticks of gum each year. And the largest gum company

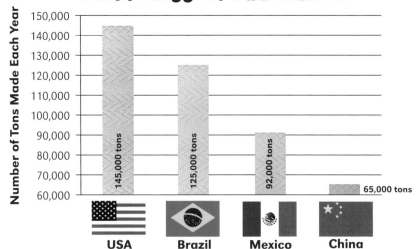

World's Biggest Gum Makers

Number of Tons Made Each Year

150,000
140,000
130,000
120,000
110,000
100,000
90,000
80,000
70,000
60,000

145,000 tons
125,000 tons
92,000 tons
65,000 tons

USA   Brazil   Mexico   China

is American. U.S. gum makers produce about 1.74 trillion sticks of gum each year. That's trillion with *T*!

During World War II, U.S. soldiers shared American gum around the world. They passed it out to make friends!

During World War II, many U.S. troops went by boat to countries in Europe and Asia. The trips were long! The soldiers were given gum to keep from feeling seasick.

This sweet treat is banned in Singapore

People in Singapore don't need to worry about stepping in gum!

It's a fact: Chewed gum belongs in the trash. Old gum that is stuck on a desk or street is gross. In the country of Singapore,

ASIA

SOUTH CHINA SEA

← **Singapore**

N
W · E
S

it is against the law to even chew gum. That ensures the gum will not end up where it does not belong!

Have you ever had gum in your hair? If so, you know how hard it is to get the gum out. There is a way, though. Dip the gummy hair in salted water and then rub it with ice. Then you can remove the gum.

Gum does not
stay in your stomach

You may have heard the old saying about chewing gum: "If you swallow gum, it will stay in your belly for

Don't worry! Swallowed gum won't live in your stomach forever!

seven years." That is not true! Swallowed gum ends up where most food does. It comes out of the body as waste.

How long does gum last in a wrapper? No one knows for sure. In fact, gum does not have an expiration date. It can get dry and hard, but it is still OK to chew.

People make "A-B-C" art

In a town in California, there is an alley where people go to stick gum on the walls. It is called

Does this look like somewhere you would want to visit?

Bubblegum Alley! The walls are filled with colorful wads. It is a masterpiece of A-B-C art. (That is short for "Already Been Chewed.") And let's face it: It is a little gross, too!

Why doesn't rain wash gum away? Gum is made of chains of **molecules**. They stretch, which makes gum chewy. That is also why gum is hard to clean off.

Activity

Can Gum Help You Concentrate?

Try this activity to see if chewing gum helps people do better on tests.

You Will Need:
- ✔ paper
- ✔ pens or pencils
- ✔ gum
- ✔ an even number of people to take part

1 Make 10 sets of four numbers, like the ones on the right, using the numbers 1 through 9.

1-5-9-2	2-3-5-8
9-2-1-7	1-8-2-4
8-3-5-7	5-2-8-1
4-6-8-7	3-7-2-9
6-2-4-9	7-5-8-3

2 Give half of the people gum to chew. The others get no gum. Explain that you will read the numbers out loud. Then ask everyone to write the numbers in reverse order on a piece of paper.

3 Read the first set of numbers slowly. Wait for your subjects to write their answers. Then read the second set. Repeat until you have read all 10 sets.

4 When everyone is done, have each person write GUM or NO GUM on the paper. Then collect the sheets.

5 Count the right and the wrong answers. Use a chart like the one below. Which group had more right answers?

	Player 1	Player 2	Player 3	Player 4
	GUM	**GUM**	**NO GUM**	**NO GUM**
RIGHT ANSWERS	6	8	5	7
WRONG ANSWERS	4	2	5	3

In this experiment, the people who were chewing gum had more right answers (14) than the people who were not (12).

Timeline

The first sugar substitute, saccharin, is made by accident during experiments with coal tar.

1848 ▸ **1879** ▸ **1884** ▸ **1928** ▸

John B. Curtis invents State of Maine Pure Spruce Gum.

Thomas Adams makes Black Jack gum.

Walter Diemer makes the first successful bubble gum.

With sugar supplies low, people in the U.S. start to use saccharin in tea and coffee.

World War II begins.

World War II ends.

| 1939 | 1940s | 1945 | 1950s | 1974 |

Sugar-free gums are introduced.

Willie Mays gets the world's largest piece of gum.

Glossary

energy (EN-ur-jee): power that makes people or machines work

molecules (MAH-luh-kyoolz): smallest units that a chemical compound can be divided into that still display all of its chemical properties

primates (PRY-mayts): members of the goup of mammals that includes monkeys, apes, and humans

resin (REZ-in): sticky substance that oozes from some trees and plants

Index

About the Author

Jessica Cohn has written and edited many dozens of books, often while chewing gum! She lives in California with her family. She enjoys hiking, helping student writers, and exploring the countryside.

Facts for Now

Visit this Scholastic Web site for more information on chewing gum:
www.factsfornow.scholastic.com
Enter the keywords **Chewing Gum**

Library of Congress Cataloging-in-Publication Data

Names: Cohn, Jessica, author.
Title: 10 fascinating facts about chewing gum! / by Jessica Cohn.
Other titles: Ten fascinating facts about chewing gum!
Description: New York, NY : Children's Press, an Imprint of Scholastic, Inc., [2017] | Series: Rookie star | Includes index.
Identifiers: LCCN 2016003494| ISBN 9780531228166 (library binding) | ISBN 9780531229415 (pbk.)
Subjects: LCSH: Chewing gum—Miscellanea—Juvenile literature.
Classification: LCC TX799 .C64 2017 | DDC 641.3/38—dc23 LC record available at http://lccn.loc.gov/2016003494

Produced by Spooky Cheetah Press
Design by Judith Christ-Lafond

© 2017 by Scholastic Inc.

Photographs © cover: Ron Nickel/Media Bakery; cover-back cover background: stock09/Shutterstock, Inc.; back cover: S. Miroff/Shutterstock, Inc.; 2: Dean Fikar/Shutterstock, Inc.; 3 left: S. Miroff/Shutterstock, Inc.; 3 right : joebelanger/Thinkstock; 4-5 background: JenD/iStockphoto; 5 top: OlegDoroshin/Shutterstock, Inc.; 5 bottom: Comstock/Media Bakery; 6 left: Maria Arts/Shutterstock, Inc.; 6 right: Doug Coldwell/Wikipedia; 7: iFry/Thinkstock; 8 left: MariuszBloch/Thinkstock; 8 center: evgenyb/Thinkstock; 8 right: joebelanger/Thinkstock; 9 bottom left: verdateo/Fotolia; 9 bottom center: scisettialfio/Thinkstock; 9 bottom right: Mamuka Gotsiridze/Thinkstock; 9 top: Comstock/Media Bakery; 10 left: Africa Studio/Shutterstock, Inc.; 10 right: anna1311/Thinkstock; 11: DeeMPhotography/Shutterstock, Inc.; 12 left: Sergiy Bykhunenko/Shutterstock, Inc.; 12 right-13 bottom: ifong/Shutterstock, Inc.; 13 top: Hogan Imaging/Fotolia; 14: Giuseppe_R/Shutterstock, Inc.; 14 background-15 bottom: MBPROJEKT_Maciej_Bledowski/Thinkstock; 15 top: Ken Wolter/Shutterstock, Inc.; 16 left: Bettmann/Corbis Images; 16 gum: Coprid/Shutterstock, Inc.; 16 -17 scale: Vicente Barcelo Varona/Shutterstock, Inc.; 17 weight: Mrs_ya/Shutterstock, Inc.; 17 right: visivasnc/Fotolia; 18 gum: Abramova Elena/Shutterstock, Inc.; 18 left: Stefanina Hill/Shutterstock, Inc.; 18 center left: Globe Turner/Shutterstock, Inc.; 18 center right: Globe Turner/Shutterstock, Inc.; 18 right: Artgraphixel/Shutterstock, Inc.; 19: Galerie Bilderwelt/Bridgeman Art Library; 21 top: Valentyn Volkov/Shutterstock, Inc.; 21 bottom: Dave Fimbres Photography/Getty Images; 22: stanfram/Thinkstock; 23 stomach: eranicle/Shutterstock, Inc.; 23 gum monster: egg design/Shutterstock, Inc.; 23 couch: Karen Katrjyan/Shutterstock, Inc.; 23 picture frame: Banana Republic images/Shutterstock, Inc.; 23 monster in frame: egg design/Shutterstock, Inc.; 23 top: OlegDoroshin/Shutterstock, Inc.; 24 left: annhfhung/Getty Images; 24 right-25 bottom: SiliconValleyStock/Alamy Images; 25 top: Africa Studio/Fotolia; 26-27 bottom: Sadeugra/iStockphoto; 27 top: ridjam/Fotolia; 28 top: NoDerog/iStockphoto; 28 bottom: Felix Choo/Alamy Images; 28 center: Sebastian Studio/Shutterstock, Inc.; 29 top: Paul MacKenzie/Shutterstock, Inc.; 29 bottom: Bettmann/Corbis Images; 30 top: MBPROJEKT_Maciej_Bledowski/Thinkstock; 30 center top: Africa Studio/Fotolia; 30 center bottom: iFry/Thinkstock; 30 bottom: Maria Arts/Shutterstock, Inc.

Maps by Jim McMahon